How to build
A BIGGER & BETTER
HYDROPONIC GARDEN
for less than $20

by
Ed Sherman
Jim Leslie
Adrienne Chan

NOLO PRESS

OCCIDENTAL
box 544, occidental, ca. 95465

Jim drew it. *
Adrienne printed it
and took pictures.
Ed had the pleasure
of their company.

Other books by Ed Sherman

How To Do Your Own Divorce in California

California Tenants Rights Handbook

Protect Your Home (Homestead)

HYDRO-STORY, A complete manual
of hydroponic gardening at home

ISBN 0-917316-18-5

© 1978 by Ed Sherman

Thanks to Helmut Julinot & City Green, Toronto
for photos on pages 15,52, back cover. And
thanks * to Sherry Margolin for drawings
on pages 34, 39, 41.

retailers contact:

HOMEGROWN SUPPLY CO.
Box 407, Occidental, Ca., 95465.

This one is for fun
and for the ones who
have made it that way.

FORWORD!

This book is the result of years of experience and a strong desire to see more folks growing flowers and food -- especially those who don't think they have the time, place or desire to do it. Here we tell you just enough about hydroponics to make you feel good and confident (maybe even enthusiastic) about doing it, but mostly this book is to show you specifically how to make one very ideal little garden -- the best one we know about. It is ridiculously cheap to set up and a giggle to grow in. It makes gardening recreational, not to mention productive and profitable.

We have another book, **HYDRO-STORY**, by the same team, which is more general and which covers hydroponics in more breadth and detail. It can be regarded as a companion to this one (though either will stand alone) so we blushingly recommend it to you. If your library doesn't have one, first file a complaint, then after demanding it from your local bookstores and nurseries you may then turn to the inside back cover for ordering instructions.

TABLE of CONTENTS :

Water, earth, air & sun

~ to grow, you sow ~

How simple it all really is.

Telling you how to grow
a plant
is like telling you how
to make love —
It's very personal
and a lot of
different things work.

WHY HYDROPONICS?

BECAUSE,

WE LIVE IN A WORLD WHERE THERE IS...

NO GOOD FOOD

Clean, pure, wholesome and nutritious food (not to mention flavor) is less and less available. The time is near upon us when health and happiness will absolutely require extra money to buy quality food or extra time to work a garden.

NO PLACE TO GROW

Many people prefer to or feel forced to live in dwellings without suitable garden space — they have hard, rocky soil, no soil, no room, no water, no permanent home of their own where they can build up a garden.

NO SPARE TIME

Many people prefer to or feel forced to live lives which leave too little time or energy to spare for a garden — a conventional garden, that is!

NOT MUCH SENSE

Far distant future heads will look back and wag over the quaint and unusual circumstances which caused a widely desired and very beautiful weed to become a battleground and have a black market value of over $2000 per pound; whereas the equally beautiful, and in its own way equally valuable broccoli or Chinese pod pea is worth less than $2 per pound.

THEREFORE!

WE TURN TO HYDROPONICS BECAUSE...

Hydroponics can produce clean, pure, wholesome, tasty and nutritious, food, far superior to what is NOW available at markets and permanent fruit stands.

(and)

Hydroponics is very easy to succeed at, even for first-time or spare-time gardeners. No digging, weeding, cultivating, mulching, etc., so you spend most of your time watching, pruning and consuming.

(and)

Hydroponics can produce abundantly from a small, compact, light-weight portable garden which takes minimum time to operate. You can have a recreational homestead on your apartment balcony or a permanent salad decorating your window. You can also do it to advantage in larger yardsize spaces, but that's in the other book.

(and)

Hydroponics can produce in balconies, patios, verandas, porches, window boxes, side-yards, rooftops or EVEN IN A CLOSET. It is perfect for city apartments and mobile homes. (so)

Hydroponics is very useful to the country gentleperson. It is essential to the very busy people and/or lazy people of liesure. It rescues renters, since if you have to move, you can pick it up and take it with you.

BUT

For those of you who have lots of time, energy, good soil, enthusiasm, determination and know-how, we want you to know that

WE GREATLY ENJOY OUR ORGANIC GARDEN, TOO!

Hydroponic Homestead
on a Toronto balcony

These young giants are growing in a
hydroponic bubbler garden only 14" wide by
22" long, with only 3½" of growing medium,
yet they soon doubled in size to nearly
14 ft.. Salad greens are thriving at their
feet, keeping the gardener nourished
while he waits for the big harvest.

Here's a side-yard hydroponic food factory, about 10' x 12', full of life, nourishment and fun for the family that built it. We wish we knew who the lady is, to thank her for posing for this picture.

Timothy inspecting winter peas and beets which grew completely untended (we were on vacation) from late November to early February (photo February 14th). Is that automatic and easy enough for you?

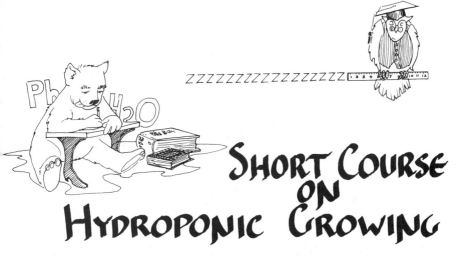

SHORT COURSE
ON
HYDROPONIC GROWING

In spite of the complicated sounding name, hydroponics is a simple thing. It merely means that you put a good diet of plant nutrients in the water instead of making the plant seek out the nutrients from surrounding soil. Think of indoor house plants — once potted, they soon use up all the nutrients in their little bit of dirt. If you don't feed them they go hungry and don't do well. If you do feed them, you are operating a simple and crude hydroponic system.

Since a hydroponic plant does not depend upon soil for nutrients, and since soil is not otherwise the best growing medium, hydroponic plants are usually grown in gravel or some similar inert substance that breathes well.

As with any method of growing, it is your plants' needs and well being that dictates what works and what does not work. Find out what they like and provide it consistently and lovingly. To do this, and to better understand how hydroponics works, it helps to know a little about the plant growth process.

 ## HOW PLANTS GROW

Living things are made up of cells. In plants the cells are engaged in a process as organized, intricate and marvelous as can be found in any other living things.

The basic requirements for good plant growth are light, air, water, inorganic mineral salts (nutrients) and good root support. The plant takes in nutrients by a process called 'osmosis' and uses light to transform water and nutrients into new cells by a process known as 'photosynthesis'. Let's look at these elements one at a time.

LIGHT

Plants require sun energy (light) to turn water and nutrients into new cells. Each healthy green leaf is a little factory using photosynthesis to turn out food and materials for the rest of the plant. This is nature's own solar energy collection and storage system. Obviously good light is essential for your plants, although some have a preference for more light than others. Most of the vegetables do better in strong light, but if you have modest light available, you can

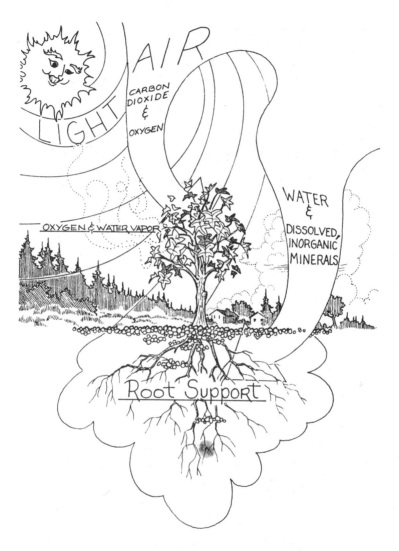

LIGHT

AIR

CARBON DIOXIDE & OXYGEN

WATER & DISSOLVED, INORGANIC MINERALS

OXYGEN & WATER VAPOR

Root Support

become an expert on growing in poor light conditions. Start off with lettuce and Chinese pod peas and other winter crops. If you are stuck with very bad light conditions, you can always try a salad garden under grow lights.

OSMOSIS

Unlike animals, plants cannot ingest or digest organic matter because they have neither mouths nor stomachs. Instead, plants 'eat' by a process known as osmosis, whereby the cells of the plant take in molecules of gas, water or inorganic minerals **directly** through the walls of the cells. Organic molecules are too large and too complicated to pass through or be used directly. In soil, enzymes, bugs and bacteria break down organic matter into simpler inorganic minerals which the plant can use. In hydroponics, the inorganic minerals are supplied directly via the water.

AIR

The greatest part of your plant's food is carbon, taken from the carbon dioxide in air. Air enters the plant through tiny pores (stomata) on the under sides of leaves. Polluted, dirty, greasy or smoky air tends to injure and clog these pores and impede plant growth. Once air enters the plant it diffuses through the spaces between the cells, dissolves into the liquid there (sap), then circulates throughout the plant giving each cell a chance to take some in by osmosis. By a reverse process gases are given off and passed back into the atmosphere.

In addition to the air taken in through the leaves, a lot of air is taken in by the roots, especially at the root crown. **IT IS ESSENTIAL** that the roots be able to breathe, otherwise the plant will suffocate and do poorly or die. Therefore the root support must not be too fine, too dense or too soggy. It must be damp, yet contain plenty of air in porous pockets. This is one of the main causes of failure in home growing! The bubbler system used in our Bigger & Better Garden automatically solves this problem.

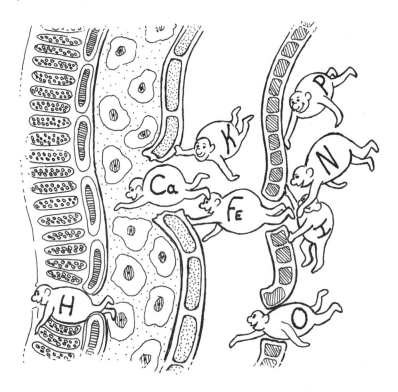

WATER

A plant is made up of as much as 90% water. Water is taken up by the roots, rises by capillary action, fills out the plant and circulates through it, eventually passing off through the leaves as a vapor. Too much water at the roots can cause the plant to drown, but insufficient moisture will slow down its vital process and cause it to wilt or even die. Water in the plants carries around the nutrients dissolved in it and also supplies hydrogen and oxygen as nutrients.

Any water good enough to drink is almost certainly good enough to grow in. In some areas, however, water is so very heavily chlorinated that you may want to let it sit for a day before using it. If you are uncertain about your water quality, go out and cut some fresh flowers and put them in some of the questionable water. If the flowers hold up for a few days then the water is okay.

NUTRIENTS

Apart from carbon and oxygen taken from air, and hydrogen and oxygen taken from water, the plant gets all the rest of its essential nutrients in the form of inorganic mineral salts dissolved in moisture around its roots. In soil gardening the inorganic minerals can come from fertilizers or from the breakdown of organic matter by soil, bacteria and enzymes. In hydroponic gardening these nutrients are put directly into the water by the gardener. This is simple, direct and easily controlled.

Nearly a dozen different minerals absolutely must be present to provide a top quality diet for your plants. The Menu shows a list of these essential nutrients and what they do for the plants.

Menu For Healthy Plants (A la Carte)

M **A** **J** **O** **R** **E** **L** **E** **M** **E** **N** **T** **S**	**Nitrogen** [N]	A major component of protein & chlorophyll. Needed for healthy, green foliage.
	Phosphorous [P]	Part of several organic acids. Promotes root action, early ripening, fruiting. Migrates to young, growing parts.
	Potassium [potash] [K]	Important to carbohydrate formation, hardening of tissues. Helps resist diseases and improves fruiting. Migrates to the young, growing parts of plants.
	Calcium [Ca]	Stimulates root growth, strengthens cell walls, assists in absorption of potassium and other ions.
	Magnesium [Mg]	Part of chlorophyll molecule. Migrates and helps in migration of phosphorous to young, growing parts.

M **I** **N** **O** **R** **E** **L** **M** **E** **N** **T** **S**	**Iron** [Fe]	Essential to formation of chlorophyll, protein synthesis and respiration.
	Sulphur [S]	Works with phosphorous, promotes growth of beneficial bacteria, aids protein production. Essential to nodule formation on legume roots.
	Zinc [Zn]	Essential, but its role is uncertain.
	Manganese [Mn]	Works with nitrogen, improves keeping quality of produce, accelerates growth.
	Copper [Cu]	Aids in chlorophyll production and respiration; resists certain diseases.
	Boron	Aids high yield, cell division. Aids protein synthesis.

Other minerals are required for plant growth, but only in such exceedingly small quantities that needs are invariably supplied by trace impurities in either the water supply or plant food. These "micro-nutrients" are of interest mainly to research scientists.

HOW HYDROPONICS WORKS

Take a container, fill it with an inert growing medium, plant it, keep the roots moist with nutrient solution and then stand back! That's hydroponics.

THE CONTAINER

The container can be any size and shape, but it MUST be made of non-toxic material. Galvanized metal would poison your plants, as would some substances which you might use to paint or seal your container (such as lead-base paint), so be careful. You can safely use wood, plastic, concrete, roofing felt, mud, clay, fiberglass, jars, pots, boxes, barrels, non-galvanized tin buckets, and so on. For sealing or painting the inside you can use asphalt emulsion, any non-lead base enamel, or epoxy paint. Let the paint cure several days before putting growing medium in.

The growing medium should be at least 4 inches deep, preferably 6 and as much as 8 or 10 would be good.

THE MEDIUM

The growing medium we prefer to use is plain common pea gravel. This is small gravel screened to about 1/8 to 1/4 inch in size, available at many building supply centers. You can also use coarse sand mixed with fine gravel, broken brick, baked shale, or even plastic styrofoam beads for the ultra-light weight installation on your carport roof. DO NOT use sand or gravel taken from near the ocean, as accumulated salts in the pores will poison your plants.

NUTRIENTS

This is the most important part of the whole hydroponic process. You will need a small (one pound) supply of a high quality hydroponic plant food, one which supplies a full and balanced diet for your plants. Too many of the commercial plant foods supply only the three major nutrients (Nitrogen, Phosphorous and Pottasium = NPK) but do not have the minor or trace elements. Read labels! Get one which has an analysis showing the presence of all the minerals listed in the MENU FOR HEALTHY PLANTS above.

If you read our companion book, HYDRO-STORY, you will find a lot more information on nutrients, including instructions for how to mix your own nutrients from bulk fertilizers (very economical) and how to mix up an organic nutrient soup from natural substances.

If you have a hard time finding a high quality plant food, write to:

HYDRO FRESH FARM
Box 511
San Martin, Ca. 95046

HYDRO-GARDENS (Chem Gro)
Box 9707
Colorado Springs, Colo. 80932

DR. CHATELIER'S PLANT FOOD
Box 20375
St. Petersburg, Fla. 33702

My high-stool sweetheart
with the Bigger & Better Garden.

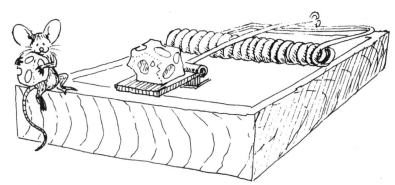

BIGGER AND BETTER THAN EXACTLY WHAT?

Yes, we did promise you a hydro garden, and a bigger and better one, too! We really mean it.

The mighty oil-drum bubbler-type garden is bigger, better and cheaper than any commercial product on the market today. It is easier to operate, more trouble free and absolutely outperforms units costing several hundred dollars. You can build your own, very easily, for less than $20. And, in case you don't like oil drums, we have other designs such as the hole-in-the-ground garden which is even cheaper, but not so handy or portable.

AS TO 'BETTER'

The most common garden being developed and produced these days for the use of the home gardener is of the pump and timer type. This is, in fact, a very good design, but it is much better suited to very large commercial sized gardens.

We rejected the pump and timer for being too cumbersome, too complicated and too expensive. Too many things can go wrong.

The technique described here, which we call the 'bubbler method,' was selected after years of experience with many other kinds of gardens. It wins hands down for simplicity, ease of operation and economy. The bubbler method was developed several years ago into an excellent mass-market product by Helmut Julinot of City Green Gardens, Toronto, Canada. Thousands of these wonderful little gardens are in operation around the world, and they have been proven to be quite effective. Unfortunately, City Green went out of business in 1977, which may prove, if anything, that it takes a lot more than a good idea and a good product to make it in the mass-market world.

The photos in this book are almost all of either a City Green garden or an oil-drum garden. Both of these gardens use approximately the same technique, the main difference being that the oil drum garden is a lot bigger and very much cheaper. That makes it better.

AS TO 'BIGGER & CHEAPER'

The oil-drum garden provides the gardener with 4.8 square feet of growing space in each half, for a total of 9.6 square feet of growing space at a cost of less than $20. That makes the cost per square foot of growing space to be $2.10. No other garden can beat that!

For purposes of comparison we priced commercial gardens and found prices from $90 to over $500. The cost per square foot ranged from $12 for a $350 kit, up to $44 for a ready-to-grow 18" x 36" garden priced at $200. The least expensive garden was one of our favorites, the City Green garden which sold for $90. It gave only 4.7 square feet of growing area, for an average of $21 per square foot. That's exactly ten times more expensive than the oil-drum garden. So the oil-drum garden is a lot bigger and cheaper, therefore better.

Two Bigger & Better gardens. The middle plant in the rear garden is the same as in the preceding photo.

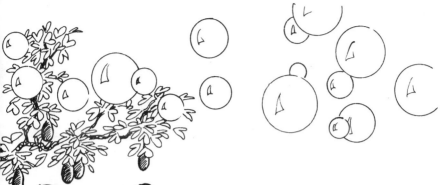

Basic Principle of the Bigger & Better Garden

The goal of any hydroponic growing technique is to keep the plants' roots moist but not wet with nutrient solution. There are many good ways of doing this, including the overly popular pump and timer garden, the wick garden, drip irrigation gardens and hand watered ones. For home sized gardens none can beat the method used in the Bigger & Better Garden which we call the 'bubbler method.'

The bubbler method is based on the simple fact that air rises through water. Air passing up a submerged and slightly leaky tube will carry bubbles of liquid up the tube.

To set up a bubbler garden you need to suspend the growing medium closely above a reservoir of nutrient solution.

There are untold cheap and simple ways of doing this, a few of which will be described on coming pages.

   Use any small aquarium pump for a source of steady, gently flowing air. The air is guided through a thin plastic tube (the air feeder tube) down into the nutrient solution. There the tube is

fitted a little bit loosely into a slightly larger tube (the bubbler tube), then runs about 6 or 8 inches up it where it is held in place by a common straight pin pushed through both tubes then bent over to secure it. This creates an intentionally leaky junction.

   The junction must be arranged to lie at the bottom of the reservoir, then as the air passes up the bubbler tube it sucks up dribbles of solution and bubbles it along into the growing medium above.

   The bubbler tube must run about an inch, no more than two inches, under the surface of the growing medium. This keeps sunlight off of the tube and moisture off of the surface of the garden and thus prevents the growth of algae, which would plug things up.

Along the length of its run through the garden the bubbler tube should have 1/16 inch holes drilled clear through every 2 or 3 inches to allow the bubbles of solution to drip out.

This method is fairly ideal, as it automatically and continuously keeps your garden moist with nutrient solution, and it also aerates and circulates the solution as it bubbles and gurgles away.

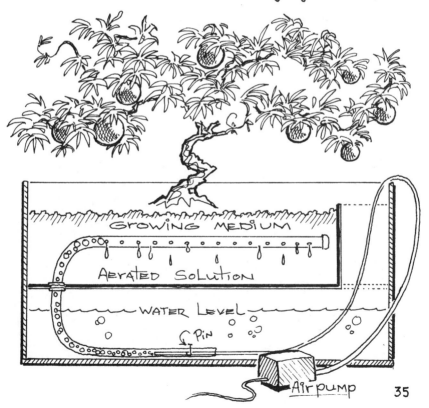

GROWING MEDIUM

AERATED SOLUTION

WATER LEVEL

PIN

Airpump

How to Build the Bigger & Better Garden

The oil drum garden is only one way to build a cheap and excellent bubbler garden. Others are suggested below and you will probably be able to think of your own. Here are step-by-step instructions for how to make the basic garden followed by suggestions for refinements and alternatives.

1. GATHER MATERIALS: Your first job is to round up a fairly clean 55 gal. oil drum. Often a little creative searching can turn one up for free, but you can buy one for $5-6 (1977 price). Call a chemical or gasoline wholesaler for hot leads. You will also need:

> One small aquarium pump (Hush I)
> 8 ft. of 1/8" I.D. plastic tube
> 9 ft. of 5/16" I.D. plastic tube
> Plastic tee connector for 1/8" tube

These items can be found at any aquarium supply counter. I.D. means "inner diameter".

Metal primer (Chex-Rust), 1 qt.
Lead free industrial enamel, 1 qt.
Assorted nails, **NOT GALVANIZED!!!**
6 cu. ft. 1/4" pea gravel, found at
brick and masonary or garden supply centers.

2. CUT DRUM IN HALF LENGTHWAYS:
This can be done with a cutting torch or
a hacksaw blade and a 1/2" drill. If you
don't have your own torch, check around
for a friendly backyard welder and make
a deal. Even a professional should do it
for just a few dollars, it's so easy.
Whoever does it should MAKE VERY SURE THE
DRUM IS COMPLETELY FREE OF COMBUSTIBLE
VOLATILE FLUIDS BEFORE USING THE TORCH,
OTHERWISE SOMEONE MAY GET SLIGHTLY
BLOWN OUT. The hacksaw method requires
you to drill holes with a 1/2" drill and
cut between them with a hacksaw blade, with
tape wrapped around one end for a handle.
(Pretend you're on a great escape adventure.)

3. FILE SHARP OR ROUGH EDGES at
least a little bit to avoid injury while work-
ing. After the garden is assembled you can
cover the edges with pieces of old hose, slit
lengthways, or with decorative wood trim.
You can leave the edges naked, but then
you should do an extra good job of filing.

4. CLEAN OUT INSIDES thoroughly
with wire brush, sandpaper, scrapers, etc.
If necessary, use soap or solvents to
remove dirt and oily deposits. The purpose
is to prepare a surface free of loose
rust, scale, and dirt, suitable for
painting.

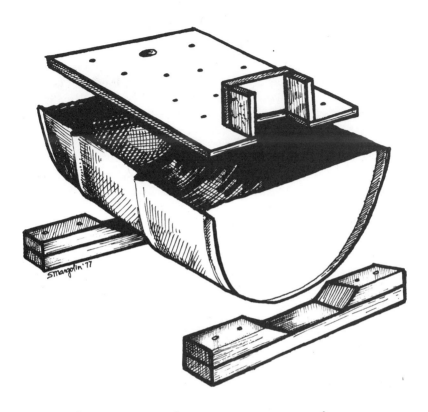

Smargolin '77

5. PAINT with a base coat of rust inhibiting metal primer, such as Chex-Rust, followed by a coat of lead free industrial enamel, any color. Paint at least the inside to prevent rust in the garden, and paint the outside for decorative effect, or not at all. Dark colors absorb more warmth, which encourages growth.

6. LET PAINT CURE for at least 24 hours before putting the growing medium in. This lets paint get tougher and makes sure all poisonous vapors have evaporated from the paint and won't get into your garden.

7. BUILD PARTITIONS: Because of the inward taper of the oil drum sides, the partitions will sit high or low depending upon how wide you cut the partition. Measure and cut carefully to get just the right width at the half-way level in the drum. You need to use material strong enough, or well enough braced, to support more than a few pounds of gravel across 22" of width. We use 1/2 to 3/4 inch exterior plywood, or thinner plywood with slats nailed on for braces. You could also piece together a partition out of slats of scrap boards, held together with a wood strip on each side. **DO NOT USE GALVANIZED NAILS** AS THEY WILL POISON YOUR GARDEN! If the material you use is solid, you should provide drainage through it with 1/4 inch holes drilled every 4 to 6 inches. Drill a hole at one end for the bubbler tube to pass through, and cut an access hole at the other end.

The access holes should be large enough to get your hand through comfortably — it is the entryway for the feeder tube, water, nutrients, and you may want to reach in to check the junction. The access hole needs a wall around it to hold back the gravel. The wall can be made of scrap wood, an old tin can, painted to resist rust, an old plastic bucket, or anything you can find.

8. MAKE CRADLES: The drums must be held in place and prevented from rolling. You can wedge them with brick, decorative stones, make wooden wedges, or build an attractive cradle.

9. PREPARE FEEDER AND BUBBLER
TUBES: The air feeder tube consists of a 4 foot length of 1/8 inch plastic tubing. Once your garden gets settled in place you can trim it to the exact length necessary. Insert one end of the 1/8 inch tube about 6 or 8 inches into the 5/16 inch bubbler tube and run a pin through both of them to hold them in place. Bend the end of the pin over to keep it from slipping out.

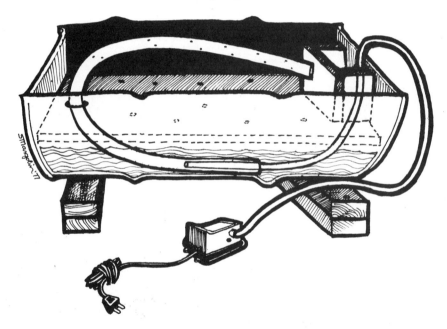

10. ASSEMBLE GARDEN: Pass the
bubbler tube up through the partition, leaving just enough below so that the junction of the two tubes can lie comfortably at the bottom of the reservoir. Run the air feeder tube through the access hole and put the partition in

place. Bend the bubbler tube over and arrange it as it will lie in the garden, and cut it to length. Drill the bubbler tube clear through every 2 to 3 inches with a 1/16 inch drill down the whole length of its run through the growing medium. Make sure the little holes are not clogged with plastic particles cut up by the drill. If you don't have a drill, burn the holes with a hot skinny nail or wire. Fill the growing bed with clean pea gravel, making sure that the bubbler tube is 1 to 2 inches below the surface of the gravel.

11. **TWO GARDENS ON ONE MOTOR** is possible if you use a little plastic tee connector right at the air pump and run two air feeder tubes off of it. BALANCE is the name of this game since you want the air to run equally through both tubes. If the water is much lower on one side the air will all tend to run out that side, since the weight of the water is lower. Keep the gardens equally topped up. You can try balancing with a set of cheap plastic thumb valves available at any aquarium store, or you may eventually wind up the owner of two or more air pumps.

REFINEMENTS & ALTERNATIVES

Now that you have seen how to build the basic garden, we want to expose you to some other possibilities. The oil drum garden is fine as it is, but a bit bare bones. If it is going to be part of your living space you may want to make it more attractive — a paint job, wood trim and an interesting cradle will give you a conversation piece as well as a garden. Or you can make it out of something other than an oil drum. Also, there are a couple of attachments you should know about that can make your garden even more flexible and automatic. Here are some ideas that will at least stimulate your thinking...

TIMER

Attaching a timer to your garden can be very convenient, useful or essential, depending on where the garden is kept. If the garden is in or near your living space, the quiet humming, bubbling and gurgling can slowly and quietly drive you nuts. A timer can turn the garden on and off to suit your quiet-time schedule. Although it works wonderfully when running 24 hours a day, this is not necessary, especially at night. Having the bubbler off for part of each day can help combat excessive dampness. This can stimulate plant growth and reduce the risk of fungus. Be very watchful and careful during hot, dry weather not to leave it off too long, especially during the day, otherwise you may wither your plants.

GROW LIGHTS

No grow light can duplicate the quality of direct sunlight. Growing outdoors or in a greenhouse is best, but lights can be a valuable growing aid to supplement poor light on the off season, or when that is all you have, or to enable you to grow inside for decorative or dramatic effect, or to maintain that secret garden in your closet, bedroom, basement or attic. When possible grow near a bright window and supplement with lights. When necessary, you can in fact get fairly good results with lights alone. You can do well enough with 4 ordinary cheap fluorescent tubes together with a couple of 15 watt bulbs, but they really don't have a rich enough spectrum. Grow lights can produce a big vigorous looking plant, but experience shows that it may lack resilience. What would be a minor disturbance to an outdoor plant can be a major setback to a plant grown under lights. That's why it pays to get the best lights available, even though they cost a lot more. As of this writing the best is the 'Vita-Lite Power-Twist' made by Duro-Lite.

STYROFOAM BEADS

For those special times and places where gravel is just too heavy or inconvenient we recommend that you try growing in plastic styrofoam beads of the sort used to stuff bean-bag chairs or to pack fragile merchandise. They should be small, less than 1/4 inch. It looks good if you cover the beads with a layer of pebbles, and this also helps hold things in place.

FLOAT VALVE

A bubbler garden is very nearly automatic except for the fact that you **MUST** keep it full of water. On hot days a full grown garden may need to be checked twice or more each day. Wide variations in water level can be survived but they are really not good for the plants. The concentration of nutrients goes through too many changes. To solve this problem we have designed a cheap little float valve that you can make for each garden which will keep it full at a constant level. It's made from a ping-pong ball, the bottle from a child's soap bubble toy, 4 inches of 1/8 copper tube, a piece of wood and a 5 gallon plastic bottle.

The float valve works from a reservoir of water just a short distance above the valve so there's not much pressure. In the valve a ball pushes against a rubber flap (old inner-tube) when the water level is up, closing off the flow water. When the level drops, more water flows in until it fills and closes itself off again.

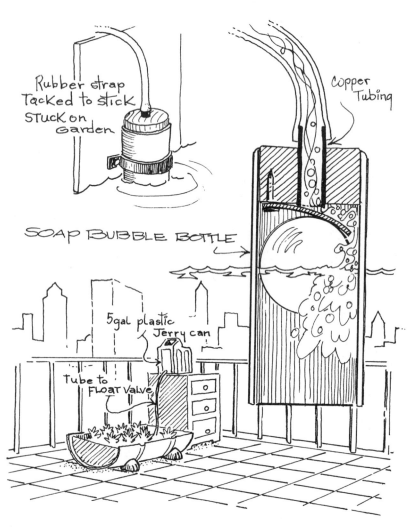

Rubber strap Tacked to stick Stuck on Garden

Copper Tubing

SOAP BUBBLE BOTTLE

5gal plastic Jerry can

Tube to Float Valve

OTHER CONTAINERS

Almost any scrap material you can lay your hands on can be made into a garden — a source of health, food, beauty, even profit. Buckets, boxes, packing crates, old tractor tires, discarded wading pools, and so on. Things that won't hold water on their own can be lined with heavy plastic (20 mil.). An old water bed would do just fine. You could even dig a hole in the ground, smooth it, grade it to drain evenly toward the access hole, and line it with plastic. A sheet of plywood held up on inverted flower pots would make a good partition. You could have the easiest, cheapest garden on the block. The challenge, and the pleasure of life is to make something creative and useful out of whatever is around you.

water pot planter made from an old plastic tub.

Garden full of legal herbs. Also a good idea for an attractive wooden, easy to build container.

A garden can be made by knocking a few boards together. This kind of wood frame can hold the reservoir if you line it with plastic, or put it over a plastic-lined hole in the ground to hold the growing medium in a raised bed. The partition can be a sheet of plywood sitting on inverted flower pots.

Schefflera in an office - here's an
an attractive bubbler-type planter
made from a plastic pot.

THE WATER POT GARDEN

In this section of refinements and alternatives we now come to the **ULTIMATE ALTERNATIVE** — a completely different way to run a hydroponic garden.

The water pot garden is even simpler than the bubbler garden, but it is not backed up by the experience of thousands of units in operation accumulated by City Green, while that company was in business. Our own experience is that they work just as well.

This garden has no partition and no bubbler tubes. You simply fill any suitable container with six to ten inches of gravel, keep the solution level at about two inches below the surface and put in your plants. Keep the solution level fairly constant. The plants breathe at their root crowns and in the upper, drier level, and the roots grow at will into the liquid to drink and eat. The solution is kept aerated and circulated by setting up aquarium air stones at the bottom before putting the gravel in. The air stone is a small piece of porous rock, and when the air from the pump passes through, it is broken up into myriad tiny bubbles which dissolve into the solution much better than would just a few big ones. The motion of the bubbles rising circulates the solution. One small air pump can operate two stones. The oil drum garden should have **at least** two stones in each side and for any larger garden use four or more.

You will need an access hole clear through to the bottom to allow you to stir in and pump out nutrients, observe the solution level and mount a float valve, if so desired. Make the access hole from a roll of hardware cloth wrapped with screen or from a piece of 4 to 6 inch plastic drain pipe drilled with lots of 1/8 inch holes to permit free circulation. The holes should be long enough to reach from top to bottom with a couple of inches left over at the top.

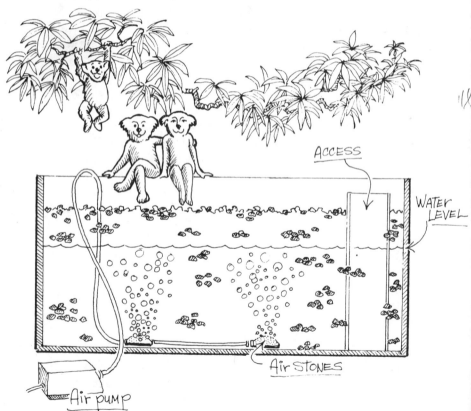

ACCESS

WATER LEVEL

Air STONES

Air PUMP

GROWING INSTRUCTIONS

There's a lot to say about hydroponic growing technique but not much room here to say it in. Naturally, we recommend that you read our companion volume, <u>HYDRO-STORY</u>, which has a broad treatment of the subject together with growing notes on most of the common garden vegetables. Also, if you are going to specialize in growing one particular kind of plant, such as indoor tropicals or marijuana, it would be very good to read the general literature about your favorite. Meanwhile, we include here some condensed hi-lites to get you started growing and getting maximum yield (and you can, indeed, get a lot) from your small growing space.

GETTING STARTED: First, find out the capacity of your reservoir: Fill it up with water, then pump or siphon it back out into a gallon jug and see how many times you fill the jug up before the tank runs dry. Use a short length of old garden hose for a siphon - anything thinner takes forever to empty out a large tank. Add the required amount of nutrient to the reservoir (read the label, usually one teaspoon per gallon) then fill with water, stirring with the stream as you pour it in.

The nutrient solution is good for at least three weeks in a fully developed fast-growing garden, and at least six weeks in a new or slow-growing garden. So, every 3 to 6 weeks you should empty out the old solution (on lawn, flowers or trees, please, as there's a lot of good stuff still in there) and put in a fresh batch. In between times **IT IS IMPORTANT** that you keep the reservoir pretty well topped up with water at all times. Here's why: Plants drink the water a lot faster than they use the nutrients, so as the water level goes down the solution becomes more and more concentrated since there's the same amount of nutrients in a smaller quantity of water. Pretty soon the solution gets too salty and this is not good for your plants. Watch your garden carefully, especially during hot dry weather when a fully developed garden may need to be topped up a couple of times a day. Or make a float valve (p. 48) and keep it automatically topped up at all times.

PLANTING: Some seed, especially the larger ones, can be sown directly into the garden, but little ones may have an unpredictable time of it in the coarse gravel. With small hydroponic gravel gardens you can generally get better results by transplanting. This way you can start lots of seeds and use only the very best of the seedlings that you raise. An average seedling will most likely grow into an average adult plant, not to be despised, but why bother with less than the best?

Start seeds in individual little pots with inert material such as perlite, vermiculite, coarse sand, etc. **DON'T** put dirt into your garden - it harbors disease. The little starter pellets are handy and convenient and can be planted directly.

Transplant seedlings when they get two or three sets of true leaves. Don't wait until they get really big, because the older the plant, the greater the shock of transplant. The microscopic root-hairs get disturbed, injured, and the roots cannot take up moisture and nutrients well enough to support the larger plant above. Be very gentle when you transplant and try to disturb the roots as little as possible. Even with care, your transplants are likely to slow down or do poorly for one or two weeks, until the roots settle in. To transplant in your garden, simply push the gravel aside, making a hole right down to the partition (bubble garden) or slightly into the water (water-pot). Gently and carefully push the gravel back around the plant, burying it up to but not over the first set of true leaves.

STRATEGY: To get the most out of your small space you have to plot on it. Planning and experience are both useful, so until you can get some experience here are some pointers to guide your planning:

a) Spacing can be very dense. Hydroponic plants don't need much root room, so your main limitations are above the bed where the plants will compete for light and air.

    b) Pruning is very helpful, since if you keep older leaves and excess branches off you will increase light and air available to all the plants in the garden.

    c) Grow tall plants in the rear of the kind which can be trained up and away from the garden, onto strings or a trellis. In front and on the sides, put in plants which can spill over and run on the ground. This leaves the middle free for plants of short to middle height. Avoid squat, bushy plants. One good zucchini bush can produce enough to make a lot of people sick of squash, but it will take up most of one garden, so you won't get much variety unless you can run other gardens (a brilliant idea, that!).

    d) Grow shade lovers at the base of larger plants.

    e) Plant a fast growing crop like lettuce and radishes right over a slow to grow crop like carrots and beets. Harvest quickly, making sure to clear the way for the second crop, and you can be eating salads while the roots are getting going.

    f) If you are growing marijuana, no more than two per garden, one at either end. Pray for females.

TROUBLE SHOOTING

The most important way you can avoid trouble, and to catch it early if it happens, is to watch your plants and learn to watch them ever more sensitively. This is the heart of what is meant by 'caring' for them. The goal of growing is the plants' well being. They are your most sensitive indicators of trouble, if you can only learn to watch them more sensitively. Hopefully, you will notice changes early and not just as the plant is about to expire.

Hydroponics is relatively trouble-free when just a little care is taken. If you use a good nutrient in the manner recommended by the maker, and if you keep the reservoir regularly topped up, then very little is likely to go wrong.

If your plants mysteriously start to look poorly, then consider these possibilities: too hot; poor light; frost; roots waterlogged; poor ventilation (with enclosed plants); toxic material in the system (galvanized pipes up the line, cat pee from trespassing feline, etc.); pests, such as mites, spiders, white fly, or aphids. If none of these appear to be at fault, then you should suspect and **IMMEDIATELY TREAT FOR FUNGUS!**

Because hydroponics maintains a nice, warm and constantly moist environment, fungus has a good place to get started, and once started it can spread rapidly. Keep your operation as clean as possible, and at the first sign of **unexplained** trouble affecting the whole garden use a good fungicide, such as 'Captan'. Always have some on hand, just in case.

First pump out the reservoir, then flush the gravel with fresh water, then pump it out again. Then flush with Captan, used as directed on the label. Let stand, then fill with water through the access hole and leave it alone for a day or two. If necessary, repeat. When the plants improve, flush the garden, fill with nutrient solution and return to normal operation. Captan is said to be non-toxic to plants and animals is used as instructed. We recommend such fungicides only because there is nothing else that will for sure save your garden in case of fungus.

COMMON TROUBLE
& LIKELY CAUSES

WILTING:
- ☐ Too dry
- ☐ Too hot
- ☐ Waterlogging

PALE LEAVES;
SPINDLY GROWTH:
- ☐ Too little light
- ☐ Too hot
- ☐ Too moist or humid
- ☐ Underfeeding

BROWN MARGINS OR
SPOTS ON LEAVES:
- ☐ Hot, dry air
- ☐ Overwatering
- ☐ Sunburn
- ☐ Overfeeding

PLANT GROWING SLOWLY
OR NOT AT ALL:
- ☐ Too cold
- ☐ Underfeeding
- ☐ Overwatering

YELLOWING OF LEAVES
FOLLOWED BY LEAF FALL:
- ☐ Overwatering
- ☐ Dry air
- ☐ Cold winds

YELLOW LEAVES WHICH
REMAIN FIRM & HEALTHY:
- ☐ Water or aggregate
  too alkaline
- ☐ Very hard water supply

ROTTING OF LEAVES
AND STEMS:
- ☐ Disease, fungus
- ☐ Overwatering
- ☐ Excess humidity

DROPPING OF BUDS
AND FLOWERS:
- ☐ Dry air
- ☐ Overwatering
- ☐ As for Leaf Drop

SUDDEN DROPPING
OF LEAVES:
- ☐ Shock
- ☐ Sudden temp. change
- ☐ Sudden light change
- ☐ Cold winds
- ☐ Dry air
- ☐ Overwatering

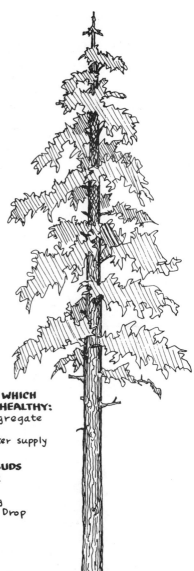

FRee PRizes for PhoToS

What's going on out there? We really want to know!

In order to find out, and in order to illustrate future ads and publications, we are offering rewards for any photographs of your hydroponic projects, gardens, ideas or crops that we decide to keep for future use. In addition to the prizes listed below, you will, of course, win our undying gratitude.

1st Prize - An Intermatic Garden Timer

2d Prize - A Hush I Air Pump

3d Prize - One Pound of Hydro Nutrient

4th Prize - Our letter of thanks, signed.

5th Prize - Your photo returned in a plain, unmarked envelope.

Let us heaR From you soon! WriTe to:

NOLO PRESS
Box 544
Occidental, Ca. 95465